Science Kids
Seasons

Winter

Aaron Carr

www.av2books.com

LET'S READ
AV²
BY WEIGL™
ADDED VALUE • AUDIO VISUAL

Go to **www.av2books.com**, and enter this book's unique code.

BOOK CODE

Y70381

AV² by Weigl brings you media enhanced books that support active learning.

AV² provides enriched content that supplements and complements this book. Weigl's AV² books strive to create inspired learning and engage young minds in a total learning experience.

Your AV² Media Enhanced books come alive with...

Audio
Listen to sections of the book read aloud.

Video
Watch informative video clips.

Embedded Weblinks
Gain additional information for research.

Try This!
Complete activities and hands-on experiments.

Key Words
Study vocabulary, and complete a matching word activity.

Quizzes
Test your knowledge.

Slide Show
View images and captions, and prepare a presentation.

... and much, much more!

Published by AV² by Weigl
350 5ᵗʰ Avenue, 59ᵗʰ Floor
New York, NY 10118

Website: www.av2books.com   www.weigl.com

Library of Congress Control Number: 2013934648
ISBN 978-1-62127-495-7 (hardcover)
ISBN 978-1-62127-501-5 (softcover)

Printed in the United States of America in North Mankato, Minnesota
3 4 5 6 7 8 9 0   17 16 15 14

032014
WEP060314

Senior Editor: Aaron Carr
Art Director: Terry Paulhus

Weigl acknowledges Getty Images as the primary image supplier for this title.

SCIENCE KIDS
Seasons
Winter

CONTENTS

There are four seasons in a year.
Winter is one of the seasons.
It is the coldest season of the year.

Fall

Winter

Winter comes after fall
and before spring.

Summer

Spring

Winter comes when the Earth faces away from the Sun. This means less heat from the Sun gets to the Earth.

Days are shorter in the winter than they are in other seasons. The first day of winter is the shortest day of the year.

Winter days are very short near the North and South Poles. There may only be a few hours of daylight each day.

Many parts of the world get snow in the winter. Snow is rain that is frozen by cold winter air.

Every snowflake has a different shape.

14

Most plants stop growing
in the winter.
This means there is less food
for animals to eat.
They have to dig under the snow
to find food.

Some animals sleep
through the winter.
This is called hibernating.

Raccoons, squirrels,
and some bears hibernate.

Some animals change color
for the winter.
The arctic fox changes
from brown to white.
This helps it hide in the snow.

Arctic foxes also grow thicker fur
to stay warm in the winter.

19

Winter is too cold to grow food outside. People use buildings called greenhouses instead. Greenhouses trap heat inside to help plants grow.

21

Winter Quiz

Test what you have learned about winter. Winter is the coldest season of the year. What signs of cold weather do you see in these pictures?

KEY WORDS

Research has shown that as much as 65 percent of all written material published in English is made up of 300 words. These 300 words cannot be taught using pictures or learned by sounding them out. They must be recognized by sight. This book contains 72 common sight words to help young readers improve their reading fluency and comprehension. This book also teaches young readers several important content words, such as proper nouns. These words are paired with pictures to aid in learning and improve understanding.

Page	Sight Words First Appearance
4	a, are, four, in, is, it, of, one, the, there, year
5	after, and, before, comes
7	away, Earth, faces, from, gets, means, this, to, when
8	days, first, other, than, they
11	be, each, few, may, near, only, very
12	air, by, different, every, has, many, parts, that, world
15	animals, eat, find, food, for, have, most, plants, stop, under
17	some, through
18	also, change, grow, helps, white
20	people, too, use
22	about, do, pictures, see, these, what, you

Page	Content Words First Appearance
4	seasons, winter
5	fall, spring, summer
7	heat, Sun
11	daylight, hours, North and South Poles
12	rain, shape, snow, snowflake
17	bears, raccoons, squirrels
18	arctic fox, color, fur
20	buildings, greenhouses, heat, inside, outside
22	quiz, signs, weather